D0783621

HOUSE ARREST

HOUSE ARREST

ALAN BENNETT

faber P PROFILE BOOKS

First published in 2022
by Faber and Faber Limited
74–77 Great Russell Street
London WC1B 3DA
and
Profile Books Ltd
29 Cloth Fair
London EC1A 7JQ

Typeset by Agnesi Text, Hadleigh, Suffolk
Printed and bound by Clays Ltd, Elcograf S.p.A.

Illustration of Alan Bennett's desk © Jon McNaught

A selection of these diary entries was first published in the
London Review of Books (7 January 2021) and then in
House Arrest: Diary Selections from a Pandemic Year
(LRB Limited Editions, 2021)

The right of Alan Bennett to be identified as author
of this work has been asserted in accordance with Section 77
of the Copyright, Designs and Patents Act 1988

A CIP record for this book
is available from the British Library

ISBN 978–1–800–81192–8

HOUSE ARREST

PANDEMIC DIARIES

But any writer would say that, though the sales and plaudits come not with doing it but having done it, the useful medal to have would be one bestowed, as it were, on the field of battle, hung round your neck in recognition of yet another fruitless morning spent at the typewriter or after a week or even months spent staring out of the window.

– from *Staring out of the Window*
Alan Bennett, 2001

24 February Last week Rupert and his whole magazine were thrown into confusion when for no apparent reason the management enquired how many of the team could work from home. This was taken to be the prelude to some sort of shedding of staff. Today it transpires it's less inimical than this, but rather a precaution. The coronavirus in Italy has meant the Milan office has had to close, the enquiry in case a similar situation should arise in London. This is thought to be unlikely.

1 March Thanks to arthritis I'm now much less mobile than I was. Gone are the days when I could jump on my bike to pop down to the shops, so static semi-isolation is scarcely a hardship or even a disruption of my routine. Himself no slouch when it came to work, George Steiner once asked a Soviet dissident how he got through so much. 'House arrest, Steiner. House arrest.' Alas, so far as work is concerned, I haven't yet noticed much difference.

The only medical scourge I've had any experience of is TB, or consumption as it was called then. The Sherwoods, a family that lived next door to us in Armley, Leeds, in the 1940s lost their youngest son to TB, which then infected his father, who also died. Unsurprisingly, this left my mother perpetually anxious lest we catch it. Mrs Sherwood was a good cook and often invited my brother and me to sample her dishes, which we were strictly forbidden to do. On one occasion, though, I succumbed (Yorkshire pudding) and foolishly saying so at home it was as if I'd signed my own death warrant.

TB was to blame for other more bizarre prohibitions. We were never allowed to wear open-necked shirts, for instance, lest the cold 'go to your chest'. Sharing a bottle of pop with other boys was another death trap, as was not wearing a vest or drinking unaired water.

TB was pretty well eradicated or controlled long before my mother's death, but she never ceased to think of it as the killer it had been in her youth. Always one to diddle her hands under the tap, she would have found the precautions against the coronavirus only common sense.

4 March HMQ pictured in the paper at an investiture wearing gloves, presumably as a precaution against coronavirus. But not just gloves; these are almost gauntlets. I hope they're not the thin end of a precautionary wedge, lest Her Majesty end up swathed in protective get-up such as is worn at the average crime scene.

Jeremy Musson the architectural historian writes to me for any thoughts I might have about George Bernard Shaw, who has an anniversary coming up and with some refurbishment projected at his house at Ayot St Lawrence.

I talk to him on the phone, saying that I've always wished I'd written *Pygmalion*, not to mention *My Fair Lady*, but without being able to offer much more. I used to read Shaw a good deal (or at least take him out of Headingley Library) when I was sixteen – the russet-brown bindings of the texts often figuring in my borrowings. I suppose, thinking about it, that I did absorb the notion that plays were a form of action, they were meant to do things, solve problems or flag them up and this I say to J. Musson. What I see I have in common is that I always enjoy writing the introductions more than writing the plays themselves. But whereas Shaw plainly thought his prefaces were on a par with the text, my introductions are more in the way of gossip, explaining why I've written the play and the circumstances that have generated it. I don't think they are 'a contribution' as the Shavian prefaces are.

14 March As an over-seventy, I am officially exhorted to remain isolated and indoors which is to say that my usual going-on now has governmental endorsement.

18 March The York Theatre Royal's tour of *The Habit of Art*, the play about Auden and Britten that did well last year and was due to be revived for a festival in New York, has had to be cancelled. I write to the cast apologising and saying that one person who would not be washing his hands every five minutes is W. H. Auden.

20 March With Rupert now working from home my life is much easier, as I get regular cups of tea and a lovely hot lunch.

24 March A rare plane passes.

Rupert is upstairs on a Zoom call with his office who, like him, are now all at home.

Photo in the *Guardian* of a home-made sign at the entrance to Malham village telling or rather entreating the hordes of tourists to go home. In our village twenty miles or so away the car park is full and the place far busier than on a normal Sunday. So far from social distancing some of the visitors practically link arms. Still, it makes a change from brawling over toilet rolls.

26 March Around six Nick Hytner rings, highly excited. Piers Wenger (BBC's Director of Drama) has just rung him saying that though current restrictions make mounting any TV programmes difficult, he thinks it may be possible to do a new version of the *Talking Heads* monologues from 1988. Nick is ringing me (needlessly) for my permission. He comes round later and we thrash out some of the details in a conversation with him standing on the other side of the street. ('Was this how *King Lear* started, do you think?')

And now R. comes with a cup of coffee and a ginger biscuit, which is what John Dawson of Bleak Bank Farm gives the vet.

ril, Good Friday We have agreed that the
and crew in the *Talking Heads* remount
should do so for a token fee, with any profits to
be given to the NHS. I'm somewhat staggered to
find that this amounts to a million pounds, possibly more. It's no skin off my nose, as I never
expected the programmes to be repeated, but the
financial sacrifice for some of the cast and crew
will not just be notional. Astonishing though it is,
this gesture passes without notice.

Good Friday, when this year Pontius Pilate is
not the only one washing his hands.

14 April I give some basic notes about *Talking
Heads* to all the directors, who are on a Zoom call.
Some of the precedents from the first production
are particularly inappropriate. The first director
was Stuart Burge, who did Thora Hird's *A Cream
Cracker under the Settee* and my *A Chip in the
Sugar*. His method in rehearsal was to station
himself a foot or so in front of one's face, simulat-
ing the camera and remaining there throughout.
To begin with this was unnerving, particularly for
Thora who had never had to accommodate herself to such rigorous technique. But when after
a few days Stuart moved to the other side of the

room, we had got so used to him that both of us felt withdrawal symptoms. Today such proximity is out of the question, so I'm not sure my experiences are much help. I tell them if they have any queries about the scripts they are to ring and ask me but they're free to make small cuts – adjustments – so long as they don't touch the jokes.

16 April A card from Tom King with news of the tattoo of me that he had put on his arm (pictured in the Diary published in the *London Review of Books* of 3 January 2019): 'The tattoo remains popular, though bizarrely one person thought it was of Henry Kissinger. It also makes for an amusing conversation during intercourse.' This suggests the intercourse might be less than fervent, my name in itself something of a detumescent.

18 April Nick H. rings having had the first reading of the monologues he is producing, including a new one, *The Shrine*, about a woman whose husband is killed in a motorbike accident. At one point she talks about the sandwiches she used to make for him, 'wenged in a hedge somewhere'. Neither Monica Dolan nor Nick, who is directing it, have come across 'wenged', and I think it may be one of my dad's invented words. It meant – at least for him – to chuck. When my parents moved to the village, they were puzzled that they kept finding turds on the lawn. Then one day Dad was in the garden and a turd came flying through the air from next door, where the old lady had a dog. With uncharacteristic boldness Dad wenged it back (and it never happened again), but wenged remained in the family vocabulary.

23 April On St George's Day (and Shakespeare's birthday) the milk is sour, so no early morning tea and no breakfast until R. goes to the post office. I lie rather prematurely on the sofa at 11 a.m. – un-breakfasted and longing for a cup of tea – and of course not a soul about. I finish my umpteenth rereading of Andrew Barrow's *The Tap Dancer*, which, with Nancy Mitford's *The Pursuit of Love*, must be my favourite novel and one I wish I'd written.

Junk shops used to take us to out-of-the-way places – to Kirkby Stephen and Mrs Hill's kitchen shop, for instance, or Brampton, where there were a couple of shops. Back in the sixties, the same quest took me all over Islington and

Camden Town, and when I had learnt to drive it was junk shops that took me around Yorkshire. Lures they were in the sixties, junk shops. Since when, of course, the scope of junk has widened with shops scarce and car boot sales not a draw in the same way.

28 April The most one can hope from a reader is that he or she should think: 'Here is somebody who knows what it is like to be me.' It's not what E. M. Forster meant by 'only connect', but it's what I mean.

These days 'only connect' means bumping elbows.

7 May Some time in the afternoon Alex Jennings and Lesley Moors call by and we have a socially distanced chat on the doorstep, me sitting on a stool, Rupert standing behind me. They bring me a birthday present (as yet unopened), having just taken something similar to Nick Hytner, whose birthday is today. Mine is on Saturday and Alex's the day after, which is perhaps why we all get on so well (all Taureans, some would say). Nick rings later with a progress report on *T. H.* He is full of praise for the helpfulness of the *EastEnders* technicians, on the set of which at Elstree the monologues are being filmed.

Harriet Walter is doing *Soldiering On* and asked Nick H. how it was I 'did posh so well'. Short of a ready explanation he said (somewhat desperately) he thought it was because I had been a friend of Debo D. There is some truth in this in the sense that my awareness of upper-class tropes comes not from Debo but her sister Nancy, whose *Pursuit of Love* I have known ever since I first discovered it in *Majority 1931–1952* – the omnibus edition of Hamish Hamilton publications, read when I was at Oxford. 'Too many memoirs' would be another explanation (and 'some Evelyn Waugh').

8 May Today the displaced May Bank Holiday to mark the 75th anniversary of VE Day. London Live TV has a 'War Week', with a good deal about how the nation stood together 1939–45, but which can't help sounding ironic in the dawning realisation of how inadequately the government has managed the response to the virus.

9 May Faultless weather yesterday and today reveals (with crowds on Primrose Hill) how the lockdown is coming apart.

11 May Boris Johnson's address to the nation in the evening pretty pointless. 'Stay alert' meaning nothing. He's such a poor orator and speaker generally, one almost feels sorry for him, with the plainness of Keir Starmer a relief.

R. bought me for my birthday *The Stonemason: A History of Building Britain* by Andrew Ziminski, an account of a life spent patching up ancient and even prehistoric buildings, particularly in Wiltshire. It's also a history of ancient building methods and materials, particularly sarsen stones, and at one point the author painstakingly constructs a menhir of his own using the same tools and methods as his Neolithic predecessors. It's a book about landscape as much as about what our ancestors made of it and brings the past well into the present – my only regret is that it's very much centred on Wiltshire and the South East. I suppose that though Ilkley and thereabouts is strewn with Bronze Age remains, in our bit of Yorkshire further north, they're pretty thin on the ground.

A few years ago we acquired our own menhir from a brick dump in Accrington where we had gone looking for flagstones for the kitchen floor. It was a substantial granite post, half of an ancient gate with the cast-iron hinge still embedded in the side. It stands majestically at the end of the garden – an orphan now, in that the village is in the heart of overwhelmingly limestone Craven. Not quite an erratic.

I met a stonemason once, appropriately in an historic monument, the Pantheon in Rome; he must have been alone among the crowds of tourists looking at the structure with an eye as to how it had been done. Rupert was looking at it as a classical interior. I feel I was hardly looking at all, I was just thankful to be able to sit down, and my neighbour was the mason and his father to whom I talked.

12 May Yesterday afternoon Charles Walker from United Agents rings to ask if I knew (which I didn't) that Tony Cash has died. Tony and I were both in the same class on the arts side at Leeds Modern, even at one point sharing a desk. I think from Scarborough originally, his father a chef. His younger brother Bernard, who was also in the school, died young, in his twenties. Both were very musical, keen on jazz, Tony a clarinettist and a friend of Alan Cooper of The Temperance Seven. More outgoing than me, who at that time was very Conservative, Tony was on the left, may even have claimed to be a Communist – certainly not Christian, which I claimed to be. He hated school uniform since he was already a young man and wouldn't wear a school cap, sporting a modish corduroy number. He was one of the half-dozen of us who applied for Oxford and Cambridge in 1951 and he got in at St Edmund Hall. Doing National Service in the navy, he was in a different branch of the Russian Course from me and served as a coder in Germany. Though I knew him at Oxford, we next came across one another in TV where he worked for Melvyn Bragg. It was thanks to Tony I did the *Poetry in Motion* programmes, which I'm grateful for. He was talkative, enthusiastic and always appreciative. Dying in the middle of the coronavirus pandemic he is unlikely to have a memorial service which he deserves or even a funeral. I can see his boyhood cap now – it was like a slipper.

I also remember him at one of the evenings we had playing records at the St Michael's Youth Club in Headingley, when he and Alan Cooper were in hysterics at the conclusion of Beethoven's Fifth because Beethoven didn't seem to know how to end it – a difficulty that a few years later occurred to Dudley Moore and which he put to great effect in *Beyond the Fringe*.

15 May I've never been that fond of my hands. Now, much washed as we are told, they scarcely bear looking at: shiny, veinous and as transparent as an anatomical illustration. Far from the matt, solid, sensible instruments one has always hankered after. More 'artistic', I suppose. An old lady's hands, lying idle in a lap somewhere.

17 May Remember lying on my bed in the University Arms at Cambridge the afternoon of the day *Beyond the Fringe* opened in May 1961 listening to the knocking and scraping of the workmen titivating the colleges, never thinking I would remember this afternoon all my life.

30 May Someone writes to me apropos my piece on Hardy in *Six Poets*, recounting the story of Hardy getting down on his hands and knees in the middle of a flock of sheep and pretending to eat the grass in order to see what it was like to be a sheep. To the person's surprise they behaved exactly as they did in the story, gathering round to watch. A second go though was met with utter indifference.

1 June Coming to the end of *English Pastoral*, James Rebanks's second volume. It's harder to read than *The Shepherd's Life*, with the central section about the onset of factory farming not easy to take. Thankfully, though, in his own life at any rate the tide turns and Rebanks regains his grip on traditional farming and with it offers some hope, without it being 'fine writing' as so much pastoral writing is. What it is, though it's self-serving to say so, is a commentary on the last speech from *Forty Years On*: 'Were we closer to the ground as children or is the grass emptier now?'

3 June George Fenton rings. Asks where I am.
   'On the sofa.'
   'Position normal?'

20 June When from 1944 to '45 we lived in Guildford, we often ate (had to eat, the truth of it) in the British Restaurant there. This was a government canteen with pretty basic self-service school-dinner-type food. As a child, I found eating in public a delicate area, and I was always embarrassed when my parents patronised the place, though it was presumably all they could afford. It didn't take much to embarrass me, but

I was still at primary school, whereas my brother was at Guildford Grammar School, then as now quite a posh school, so with more reason to be self-conscious than me. Guildford was not short on cafés, the nicest (and in no way embarrassing) the Corona down the High Street, with a revolving drum of coffee beans in the window and an intoxicating aroma. Another was the Good Oven, where the scones were a particular favourite. In Leeds there would always have been the dietary supplement of fish and chips, and even in Guildford there were fish and chip shops. But they used oil, not the beef dripping on which we'd been brought up, and to us oil smelled disgusting and was yet another score on which 'down South' proved a disappointment.

10 July Isolation, such as it is, is beginning to rob me of speech. I had to call the optician today to explain how I'd broken the strut of my glasses, and I found myself so much at a loss Rupert had to take over. He didn't find this at all strange. I do.

17 July I have watched the recordings of the *Talking Heads* monologues, but because of social distancing I've not been able to attend rehearsals or meet the performers or the directors. I send them thank-you notes and good wishes, and today comes a lovely card from Martin Freeman, whom I don't know, but who is so good about the monologue he did (*A Chip in the Sugar*) that I want to write back and thank him, thus making it like an extract from *A Lady of Letters*, a thank-you letter for a thank-you letter. I'm so pleased with it, I carry Martin's card about with me in my pocket like a hand warmer.

19 July There are many depressing items of news in today's *Observer* but the most lowering is that, on account of his support for Brexit, Ian Botham is thought likely to be raised to the peerage.

24 July A piece in the *Times Literary Supplement* in which Mary Beard rereads and reassesses Fergus Millar's *The Emperor in the Roman World* (1977). I used to see him at Oxford, a stocky heavy-headed young man, seemingly always on his way back from squash. I knew at the time he was formidably clever and from a distance (with me it was always from a distance) fancied him rotten. On reflection, it was partly his name I found so glamorous, but at this age and with him dead,

I think I'm allowed to say that, though I must have been envious because half a lifetime later I note that when Mary Beard offers some criticism of his hit volume I am not entirely displeased. He looked not unlike the Welsh actor Ioan Gruffudd.

4 August Rupert goes upstairs to do his Pilates on Zoom. His teacher lives round the corner, but she is currently with her husband in Canada. Still, up he goes in his T-shirt and shorts as it's quite strenuous, and it makes no difference that she's on the other side of the world.

12 August A break from routine yesterday when instead of taking our constitutional, we go for a drive in the park. No longer riding a bike, I'm struck by the number of cyclists, few of them leisurely and moving in packs going at great speed and with not much consideration. We stop and sit for a while in Queen Mary's Garden – empty at 7.30. Unvisited for at least two years, it's idyllic.

13 August Big rows over A levels. I'm not sure if I would have benefited if my exam results had been based on coursework. I was a good examinee, but not much of a stayer in class. I needed an occasion before I could perform and even put on my suit for A levels (or the Higher School Certificate as it was then). It was the same at university, and I was shown my college's assessment of me a few years ago (the records are kept in the Bodleian) and pretty ordinary it was. When it came to the test in Final Schools, I managed to suggest I was cleverer than I was and had these untapped resources, which only lack of time prevented me from displaying. It was all part of showing off, which I could do right from elementary school.

16 August Every evening around eight we walk round the block – literally a three-minute walk. What in normal circumstances is one of Rupert's good habits is to pick up any stray scraps of paper to put them in the bin, and this evening on the corner of Regent's Park Road he retrieves a bit of paper which turns out to be a (previously used) tissue. He is appalled and we hasten home so that he can bin it and wash his hands. What we have not realised is that it's Thursday and our progress is hindered by a fusillade of clapping and pan-banging from the neighbours out on their balconies in celebration of the NHS. Rupert can clap (even with the noxious tissue), but I can't as I need to hold on to my walking stick. It also appears that, with me walking in the road, I am acknowledging the applause and even generating it. I try to disavow this by feebly smiling and shaking my head, but this just looks like modesty. It's an absurd and inexplicable incident.

20 August 'Robust', a favoured word of the right. It also means 'callous'.

26 August Yorkshire. When he's clearing the weed, R. finds a newt in the rill.

4 September What your work does is 'tell people you've been alive'. Lucian Freud.

8 September One phone call today, a woman enquiring if I've made arrangements for my funeral yet. At least it isn't a recorded voice.

14 September Yorkshire. The big sadness today is finding that Jane Mansergh's second-hand bookshop just off Settle Market Place has closed, and not for the duration of Covid but for good. It was a lovely shop full of unexpected treasures and absurdly cheap. Jane was a friend to the lonely and the eccentric, being herself very devout, though the main influence this had on her stock was the size of the theology section. Some books she wouldn't sell. I once asked her to look out for me any copy of *Moby-Dick*, only to find it was on her blacklist due to its subject. There were exotic finds: a privately printed edition of *The Unquiet Grave*, for instance, though nothing quite so unexpected as a presentation copy of some art book signed by Anthony Blunt that turned up round the corner in Age Concern.

15 September Much missed these shameful days is Tom Bingham, the ex-Lord Chief Justice and legal philosopher, who would have had Johnson scuttling for cover. Both from Balliol, one a credit to the college, the other not. I don't relish the dilemma of the fellows of Balliol when they are called on to dole out the prime minister's honorary fellowship. At least when it comes to his honorary degree from the university there is a precedent for a refusal, as that was one of the few slights that pierced Mrs Thatcher's hide.

20 September Sent by her biographer, Jasper Rees, a letter I wrote to Victoria Wood turning down a part in her comedy series: 'I can't face playing any more men with dusters. I don't mean I want to play Burt Reynolds parts, only somewhere between him and Richard Wattis, say – those are the parameters.'

She was a great woman, her performance of 'Let's Do It' at the Albert Hall the stuff of legend. I just hope Noël Coward was still around to see it. I first met her, almost epically, in Sainsbury's in Lancaster at the avocado counter. Her *Dinnerladies* was often sentimental, but she caught in the part of the handyman, played by Duncan Preston, the idiom of an old-fashioned working-class man, elaborate, literate and language-loving, which is, or was, more typical of the North than the more clichéd dialect-rich versions.

20 September Remember Hector's quote from *Henry IV, Part 2* which passes unnoticed in the film of *The History Boys*:

> The happiest youth, viewing his progress through,
> What perils past, what crosses to ensue,
> Would shut the book, and sit him down and die.

21 September R.'s niece Louisa at two years old is into dressing up (and so delighting her granny, Diana). Her latest accoutrement is a pair of pink dinosaur boots. Freddy, her brother, now six and very much his father Owen's son, saw the boots and said he wanted a pair 'only without the eyelashes'.

3 October Reading a piece on universities in the *TLS* brings back Richard Pares, whose last course of lectures I went to at Oxford in 1957. He was plainly dying, lecturing from a wheelchair and barely audible, with another don turning over the pages of his text. The subject would have been topical today, the influence of the sugar interest on English politics, not recounted then as it would be now in a humanitarian anti-slavery tone, but purely factually and without reproof. I did not know this at the time, but Pares had had something of a Damascene conversion, having been as an undergraduate one of the circle around Evelyn Waugh, before turning his back on frivolity for academic life. But the spectacle – and it was a spectacle – of someone giving his last breath to the study of history taught me more than any of the tutorials and lectures that I had

had at Oxford and which, in the last term before Schools, were about to come to an end.

9 October Around ten this morning the door-bell goes just when I'm in the passage – often these days I don't get there in time. It's an out-of-work boy, not with the characteristic bag, but just himself. He keeps well back, as I do, but immediately embarks on his spiel, that he's from Middlesbrough and on an employment scheme and do I want anything in the way of dusters or dishcloths. Such callers are familiar, or were until lockdown, and we've long been oversupplied. I generally get away with contributing a pound or two, though this is not easy as it provokes another spiel about him not wanting charity and that he is actually selling something – goods need to change hands. But, finding someone on my doorstep who is sharing my airspace, and with coins themselves agents of infection, I don't even attempt to buy him off and hear myself saying (absurdly), 'I'm sorry but we have the virus', a lie which the boy meekly accepts, turning away before I even get the door closed. It's his abject acceptance that stays with me, this not the first rejection he will have had this morning, though maybe none so specific.

22 October I don't always understand the poems in the *LRB*, or new poems generally, and what catches my eye in the poem 'John's & Sam's' by Steve Ely is not the poem itself but its footnote, explaining that John and Samuel Smith's breweries are located on the River Wharfe near Tadcaster, upstream from the former eel fishery of Ulleskelf. It's Ulleskelf I recognise. I know Ulleskelf or did. I have been fishing there. It was a long time ago, nearly eighty years in fact, but the boredom of the experience is fresh as ever.

My father took no interest in sport. Living at one point a stone's throw from Headingley cricket ground, Dad never encouraged my brother or me to go to a match and never ventured there himself. Sport apart, though, Dad was subject to crazes. A butcher for the Co-op, with Sunday his only day off, he would indulge in various pastimes. There was fretwork, when he perched by the fire at his little Hobbies fretwork machine, turning out toys which he sold for a few much-needed pounds down County Arcade in Leeds. There was home-made herb beer, non-alcoholic but highly explosive, which regularly demolished the scullery. Above all, there was the violin, which it's unfair to call a craze, as he was self-taught and played well all his life. And then, hopelessly, there was Bullets, a literary competition in the weekly *John Bull*, at which he never won a penny. And briefly there was fishing.

Fishing is generally thought of as a solitary pursuit. It is one of its attractions. But not in the Bennett family. If Dad was going fishing we all had to go, my brother and me and (in a brief interruption to her own craze of lampshade-making) my mother. On Sundays we often went hiking, though we never called it that, and it was far from plain from the way we were dressed: my brother and me in our school caps, Mam in her swagger coat and Dad in his 'other suit' – i.e. not the one with his greasy shop trousers. We never joined in, got the gear, looked the part, and so it was with fishing.

Even so, we had no choice but to join with what nowadays would be called 'the fishing community' and catch the fishing train from Leeds City Station first thing on Sunday morning. Like all trains during the war – this was 1941 – it was packed, my brother remembering him and me being pulled aboard while the train was still sliding into the platform. Among the seasoned (and seasonably clad) fishermen the Bennett family must have stood out, Mam especially, as there were very few female fishers. She was particularly unhappy, my brother remembers, because with the luggage racks crammed with fishing tackle, maggots drizzled down on the anglers' indifferent heads.

Our Sunday outings weren't purely scenic. In summer we picked bilberries on Ilkley Moor, in the autumn blackberries at East Keswick, and very occasionally (and more gingerly) mushrooms. In theory, fishing could have been added to this productive list, but not the way Dad did it and certainly not at his chosen location at Ulleskelf.

The Wharfe is a pretty river and in its upper reaches – at Burnsall, say, or Bolton Abbey – spectacularly so. Lower down, though, south of Harewood in the flat lands of East Yorkshire, it drifts between muddy banks and rhubarb fields and is a pretty dismal waterway. But then so is Leeds's local river, the Aire. No fish there either, but at least there was Kirkstall Abbey. At Ulleskelf there was nothing, and on the rare occasions when Dad managed to cast his line as far as the middle of the river his bait was spurned by the few fish that infested its murky depths. On the three or four trips we made there was never a solitary bite. Meanwhile, Mam sat glumly by with her *Woman's Own* while my brother and I read our comics, the float never twitching. Steve Ely's poem, or its footnote, talks of an eel fishery at Ulleskelf, but we knew nothing of this, and had Mam known that we were likely to run into one of these mysterious and dirty creatures that would have put paid to fishing straight off.

Though the train was always packed, I don't remember seeing any other fishermen by the river. Perhaps Dad was fishing in the wrong place and was too shy to ask. But these few visits were enough to stamp this patch of South Yorkshire as almost uniquely dismal. It has its historical connections. Towton, the site of the decisive battle of the Wars of the Roses, is not far away and a few years later at school I would learn that Cawood Castle (now owned by the Landmark Trust) was where Cardinal Wolsey was staying before he was taken back to Leicester, disgrace and death.

7 November Some time in the afternoon Rupert shouts down that Joe Biden has passed the line and been declared the winner in the Presidential Election and that the scourge of Trump has been lifted. Though Trump does not agree. Lynn Wagenknecht texts from New York saying there is dancing in the street and holds up the phone to let us hear the rejoicing. It should put a smile on people's faces here but there are few people about. Such relief.

8 November Watch the slimmed-down service from the Cenotaph, with HMQ keeping a beady eye on the revamped choreography. I am distracted, though, just as the ceremony is starting, when Rupert sees a fox in the garden. It's a tiny garden, and has walls (without that making it a walled garden), but with no obvious means of access for foxes. Fast asleep, the only sign of life the occasional twitching of an ear. Maybe it's the distant gun salute that wakes her (I think it's a vixen), but she reveals herself as plump and well fed, possibly pregnant. She hangs around for a bit, shoving her white nose through the trellis on top of the wall before disappearing next door. Meanwhile the wreath-laying has started, which I'm always impressed by. In the unlikely event of my being asked to lay a wreath at the Cenotaph I'd have to decline, if only because I couldn't walk the few steps backwards it requires. Not the least of the Queen's achievements is that she can still do this in her nineties.

12 November Lovely encounter this morning. Rupert goes for the paper and I walk with him as far as the seats in Chalcot Square where I sit and wait till he comes back. This morning there is a tall black guy sweeping up the leaves who warns me against sitting on the seat as it is wet. He then asks me how old I am – and I say I am as old as his grandfather. Do I remember the Second World War? I say I do – and indeed can remember the day it started. He talks a lot more, kind and smiling but my hearing aid isn't working so I can't tell all he says. Were we not in lockdown and everything else I would have shaken his hand – and I keep looking out of the window hoping he is sweeping the leaves in our street and I can take him a piece of Diana's iced ginger cake. It's put a smile on my face for the whole morning.

17 November Think of making a note of words I see but don't understand, still less use, e.g. double-down.

26 November A new biography of Graham Greene: not read, like, I have to confess, most of his work. I've been put off by the Catholicism showing through and his frequent 'rare' interviews. A darling of the Sunday papers in the 1960s, he was always said to be retiring while in fact being avid for publicity. Any misgivings I had were confirmed the only time I met him, in 1977. I had a play running in the West End, *The Old Country*, with Alec Guinness. Wordy I think it now and thin on plot, it was an account of a Foreign Office defector, now living in Soviet Russia, who is being tempted home, possibly to face the music. It had good reviews, though journalists, and even some critics, persisted in taking Hilary, the spy, to represent or be based on Kim Philby. This had never been my intention, with Auden more the model and exile the subject, though the misconception doubtless did the box office no harm.

In the course of the run, various luminaries came round after the show to see A.G., with him telling me to come myself one night as Graham Greene would be in the audience. I duly turned up, but remember little of the conversation (there wasn't much conversation to remember), my abiding memory only that Greene's was the limpest hand I'd ever shaken. Nor did he say a word about the play, for or against. It may be that as a friend and persistent advocate of Philby's, he had like some of the newspapers misidentified Alec as Philby. Whatever it was, I thought it a graceless performance. However, a few nights later, another visitor wiped away the memory. This was Coral Browne, funny, gossipy, and who had even liked the play, relating it to her own experiences in Moscow, where she had met Guy Burgess, and giving me, ready plotted, another play in *An Englishman Abroad*.

1 December A card from a friend, Paul Fincham, drawing my attention to a passage in *Kilvert's Diary* (which I thought I'd read).

New Year's Day 1882. I went to London by the midday mail. Reached 23 Gloucester Crescent at 3 o'clock. Katie ran down to open the door – prettier than ever. The Monk was gracious and he came forward with a smile and an embrace. The baby Mary is charming – blue eyes and fat rosy cheeks, quite a Wyndowe. She will be very pretty.

With its innocent delight in little girls – these were Kilvert's nieces – it's a characteristic passage from the young Victorian clergyman's diaries. But unless the street numbers have changed, 23 Gloucester Crescent is my sometime house, and the home too of the Lady in the Van, who wouldn't have liked the children at all.

Mark Bostridge tells me that Kilvert must have been visiting his younger sister Emily (Wyndowe) and her family. It's nice to think that Kilvert once called at the house. He joins a list of visitors that includes

Barbra Streisand
Kenneth Williams
John Gielgud
Vincent Price
Morrissey

To which can now be added the name of the Reverend Francis Kilvert.

2 December A litotic temperament – seeing the positive in a negative way, 'Not bad.'

3 December Reading and hugely enjoying Ferdy Mount's *Kiss Myself Goodbye* (even surviving a chapter on motor racing).

Also bucked to find myself mentioned approvingly in Shaun Bythell's stocking-filler of a book about the characters (complaining, whistling, farting) who infest second-hand bookshops. And not as a complainer, farter or whistler either.

9 December I'm sorry that this year's diary dwells so much on my physical incapacity. Farewell to the bike has to some extent meant farewell to the health that went with it, and my life is increasingly medicated. I am blessed in my passage through the therapeutic jungle by Louise, who's an ideal pharmacist, cheerful, funny and unbegrudging. It's a busy pharmacy in Camden Town, with its quota of recovering addicts and ancients like myself, to whom Louise dispenses not merely medicaments but much-needed good cheer. I'm happy to acknowledge the part she plays in my well-being. I must cost the NHS a fortune, and I'm glad that through *Talking Heads* we were able to repay some of that, if only a little. Johnson never fails to call it 'our NHS', though this offers no assurance that he won't sell it off, but one hopes that now he's lost his chum across the water there may be less of that.

15 December There were those in 1914 who believed that war was just what was needed – as a cleanser and a salutary shock. England would be the better for it. As we wait for the result of the final Brexit talks, the heirs of these fools are still with us.

24 December In the late afternoon we watch *Carols from King's*, which isn't the customary Festival of Nine Lessons and Carols. It may be that the BBC, or even King's, has got nervous about overdoing religion. The service has a dramatic shape, beginning with Isaiah and ending with the Nativity and St John. Now, or today anyway, no nine lessons but an anthology of devotional stuff, well meant but telling no tale. Christmas is a time for repetition – the repetition part of the ritual. The congregation isn't bored with Christmas, only the programme-makers.

31 December My year ends when Rupert takes me up to one of the health centres in Camden, which has been kitted out as a vaccination centre. Though neither of us knows quite where it is, we realise we must be getting close from the number of eighty-year-olds and carers making their way off the Kentish Town Road, all on the same errand. Unfortunate that both the disease and the remedy begin with a v. At eighty-six (I excuse myself), I get them mixed up so at the head of the queue for the vaccine I say it's for the virus, both of them v words. Rupert isn't allowed in, and I go fairly briskly through a series of waiting rooms before reaching the vaccination room. It's busy but quiet, and notable, considering the presence of so many aged patients, for the absence of chuntering. Everyone, not surprisingly, seems in good humour. My only complaint is that since I'm isolating with my partner, it would seem sensible to vaccinate him too. But then not all the staff at the centre have been vaccinated either.

18 January 2021 I have worn pretty much the same outfit since this business began, only varying it as the weather's got colder to put on a thicker pullover. This has something to do with not yielding to circumstance, and reminds me of fellow conscripts on the Russian Course during my National Service in 1953. It was a very relaxed unit, and we did not have to wear uniform except on ceremonial occasions and were issued with official civilian clothes, though one could wear one's own choice of outfit. One colleague refused this better option and insisted on wearing the army-issue kit, reasoning that to wear one's own clothes was to give the military something – the wear and tear on the clothes – to which it was not entitled. The army civvies were ill-fitting, itchy and unbecoming, and came from a depot at Woking – 'A Woking suit, no smoking suit' was one of the cabaret turns we did at the time.

4 February Slightly wish I'd lightened my grumblings about arthritis with a reminiscence of my great-uncle Norris, included in an earlier memoir but no worse for that. Uncle Norris was, I think, Grandpa Peel's brother and was a wine and spirit merchant by profession. He ended his days in Stafford House, an old people's home in Halifax, but very cheerfully, as he was convinced (and never missed an opportunity of telling you) that he was about to become a millionaire. Why? Because he, Norris Peel, had discovered the cure for arthritis, and once this was made known, an arthritis foundation in America would make over to him their entire funding. The cure consisted in cutting off the feet of one's socks and wearing them as anklets. This is what Uncle Norris had done and he had never had arthritis, so it must be a cure. He had written to many of the notables of the day to tell them the good news – a mixed bag: Winston Churchill, Semprini, Wilfred Pickles, Val Doonican – and he would show you a sheaf of their acknowledgments, which included several outlying royals. 'He's batchy,' Dad would say, meaning 'he's barmy', but it certainly kept him happy.

27 February The hair is getting to be a problem. As children, my brother and I had our hair cut at Mr Shaw's, the barber on Armley Moor Top in Leeds. It was a wearisome business after school when the shop was always full. Mr Shaw, who was bald, never condescended to talk to us children, who in any case were rapt in *Everybody's* and *Picture Post* and even the occasional *Lilliput*. When we lived in Headingley it was Mr Oddy on Shire Oak Street, another bald and taciturn fellow, but with classier magazines, in particular *Britannia* and *Eve*, notable for illustration of bare-breasted ladies driving chariots in the genteel porn that was the speciality of F. Matania. My dad had his hair cut on the same parade as his butcher's shop in Meanwood, though never to the satisfaction of my mother, who claimed he came home 'looking like a scraped cock'. She meant a plucked fowl, and had no thought of being misunderstood.

Today's barber is my partner, who, while professing to admire my abundant locks, manages to make me look like a blond Hitler. He was also wondering if he could have the offcuts, in case they might find a market on eBay.

11 March It should not be forgotten that, with his customary foresight and good judgement, one of the first acts of the current prime minister was to hasten to the side of President Trump, whom he then shipped across the Atlantic to meet H.M. The Queen. And that it was the now much-abused Speaker, John Bercow, who ruled out any thought of Trump addressing a joint session of parliament. His reward was to be refused the customary peerage on retirement by this prime minister, who happily doled out peerages to umpteen millionaires, all of them donors to the Tory Party. And so we go on.

The Journey Home

Now in the autumn of 2021 we have resumed our pre-lockdown routine, going home by train from King's Cross to Leeds with a wheelchair at both ends. It's an exemplary service, friendly, cheerful and sometimes hair-raising, they push you at such a rate. Today unaccountably there is a life-size dinosaur in the booking hall at Leeds, thrashing its tail and emitting great belches of prehistoric dyspepsia. Lunch follows just outside the station at Sous Le Nez, a cosy brasserie on Quebec Street where we have been coming now for ten years, and which happily has survived its enforced closure. Table 25. Fish and chips invariably. In and out in 45 minutes, after which we drive north and home.

It's always said of Leeds that it's easy to get out of, not much of a compliment though it's true, and I've been doing it half my life. In my TV play *Sunset Across the Bay* (1975), a couple retiring from Leeds to Morecombe wave the city goodbye saying, 'Bye bye, mucky Leeds.' True in 1975, it wouldn't be true today when, though too much has been demolished, at least it's clean with green fields on the horizon where once were back-to-backs.

These days it's Rupert who does the driving and like Guermantes and Combray (though not) there's a choice of routes, with Burley Road above Kirkstall the current favourite. On the left across the valley is the spire of St Bartholomew's where my parents were married, and further along the tower of Christ Church where I went to what was then called 'little school'. But now we must turn off up St Anne's Lane, a slightly awkward thoroughfare which only just takes the passage of two cars. Today someone (possibly having had a scrape) has fixed a neat cyclostyled notice to a lamp post: 'Stupid thin road.' It's the choice of 'thin' rather than 'narrow' that makes it droll.

We now cross Headingley Lane, heavily parked if the Rhinos are playing a match, and go up Queenswood Drive past a parade of shops that includes the salon Scissor's Palace. There's also a second-hand furniture shop which, lacking the onomastic ingenuity peculiar to hairdressers, is called 'Take Another Look', but which often has its stock outside on display. We have a fantasy that one day we will see a William Kent chair or something by Chippendale but in all the years we've been coming by we've never stopped to find out.

On we go, turning right into Spen Lane past the house once lived in by Mr Fletcher, the music master at my school who was an early fan of Sibelius and was once invited to Finland to meet him, only the Council wouldn't give him time off. Then down West Park Drive where somewhere lived Tolkien, the house nowadays not perhaps quite the place of pilgrimage it once was. This brings us to Otley Road and past the site of my school, Leeds Modern, and a casualty of Leeds's passion for demolition, its replacement not unlike a small provincial airport. This is the ring road with beyond it the genteel suburb of Lawnswood, with its crematorium where I used to work as a student (though only as a gardener not a stoker). Beyond Lawnswood in theory ... and until recently in fact ... is the green belt, now sadly nibbled away so that from Lawnswood to Bramhope is virtually built over. Bramhope is the home of the Brownlee brothers, the Olympic medallists (with a pub named after them) and once (and maybe still) Saddam Hussein's sister (with no pub). It's here, though, just round the corner, that one gets the first hint of Wharfedale and the beginning of the dales.

In the old days, this journey was much more stop and go than it is today, as it was enlivened by a succession of junk and antique shops. There was never much in Otley, though that did have a pub named after me, if only for a month. Ilkley had two or three good shops where one could get the odd bargain but now long gone. It was in Ilkley in 1984 that we filmed *A Private Function*, and the butcher's shop in Ben Rhydding where, in the film, the butcher (Don Estelle) was had up for selling horse meat is still a butcher's today, though presumably with superior produce.

In season the A65 is a busy road, some of the traffic headed to Burnsall and Upper Wharfedale, the rest of it en route for the Lake District. Out of season or in the evening we sometimes turn off to Bolton Abbey. Another location for *A Private Function*. Empty in winter, on a summer evening one may catch a heron fishing by the stepping stones. Then on to Draughton where much more recently there would be a vase of flowers always fresh, marking the place of an accident and which Mike Harding made into a poem and was my inspiration for the monologue *The Shrine* in last year's *Talking Heads*. Round Skipton and through Gargrave (with two antique shops still), and at Coniston Cold we cross John Carr's bridge over the infant River Aire, coming down from Malham still as bright and fresh as it is in *The Water Babies*. The first sight of Ingleborough is always memorable though, in the fifty years I've lived here, the only time I've climbed it was as a soldier on Coronation leave in 1953. If it's dark and with no street lights, the first thing one notices getting home are the stars and how high the beck. My parents first came here from Leeds in 1966 and were very happy and are still remembered. 'I don't care how celebrated you are,' the coalman said. 'You'll never be a patch on your dad.'